BEDFORDSHIRE LIBRARIES

AVALANCHE BOOKS

Published in Great Britain by Avalanche Books, England 2012

Printed by SRP, England

The moral rights of the authors have been asserted.

British Library Cataloguing in Publication Data. A catalogue record for this book is available from the British Library.

ISBN: 978 1 874392 69 9

Poetry is the music of the soul, and above all, of great and feeling souls.

Voltaire

Bedford Borough Council	
9 39602477	
Askews & Holts	
821.08	

EDITOR AND AUTHORS' NOTES

The worlds of the poet and the troubadour have always been creatively intertwined. Seductive Harmonies embraces the relationship between the two art forms which have been historically so inextricably linked.

This collection explores this fertile tradition, celebrating the rythmn, the lyricism and the inherent musical quality of poetry, as illustrated by the many traditional and contemporary pieces included here; a number of which have been written especially for performance or have been set to music.

Arguably Emily Dickinson has enjoyed the most varied musical interpretation, with her poems having been set to music by, amongst others, Copland and Simon Holt. W B Yeats has also been extensively set to music, notably by the Waterboys and Piotr Kopiński. Yeats described his poem, 'The Lake Isle of Innisfree' as being "my first lyric with anything in its rhythm of my own music"

The musical theme is continued by 'Footprints', 'How Strange the Pain' and 'Onward City Moments' by Matt Harvey, which have all been set to music; 'Wild Garlic', 'In the Light of This' and 'The City is a Drunk' by Mark Gwynne Jones which have also been set to music and the inclusion of the song lyric 'Dress and Wait' by Chris Tutton.

'Left' by Alison Brackenbury - The words found scrawled in the notebook proved to be a rhyming part from a Lincolnshire Mummer's play: a borderline between folk poetry and folk song. 'Obit' by Alison Brackenbury - The poet who said that the flute should be played by ear was Michael Donaghy.

'Play' by David Hart - Numbers 1,3,5 from All Saints Elegies are a response to Rilke's Duino Elegies which had this as an inscription from Rilke, "Loving is good too, for love is hard", Section 2 is a re-response to Liz Johnson's 'Inflorescence' her recent response for saxophone and piano for an aspect of his book-length poem of Bardsey Island, "Crag Inspector".

The popular poem 'In the Bleak Midwinter' by Christina Rossetti, 1872, was written in response to a request from the magazine 'Scribner's Monthly' for a Christmas poem, with music later added by Gustav T Holst in 1906.

Contents

Symphony, *Chris Tutton*   *11*

The Song, *John Mole*   *12*

Piano Solo, *Henry Shukman*   *13*

From River Sounding, *Mimi Khalvati*   *14*

Music I Heard, *Conrad Aiken*   *15*

Cello Suites, *Roselle Angwin*   *16*

Footprints, *Matt Harvey*   *18*

Pearl, *Myra Schneider*   *20*

The Artist at 81, *Lawrence Sail*   *21*

Italian Music in Dakota, *Walt Whitman*   *22*

52nd Street, *Linda France*   *23*

The 23.30 from London, *Alison Brackenbury*   *24*

Scottish Baronial, *Katrina Porteous*   *25*

The Day is Done, *Henry Wadsworth Longfellow*   *26*

Sunday Morning - Chichester Cloisters, *Anne Caldwell*   *28*

Heart we will Forget Him, *Emily Dickinson*   *29*

Writing to Someone Else's Music, *Hannah Silva*   *30*

Forgetfulness, *Gaia Holmes*   *32*

A Serenade at the Villa, *Robert Browning*   *33*

Nico, *John Mole*   *36*

Losing the Language, *Anne Caldwell*   *37*

Stentor Hywel, *Lawrence Mathias* 38
There Came a Wind like a Bugle, *Emily Dickinson* 39
Dress and Wait, *Chris Tutton* 40
Left, *Alison Brackenbury* 42
Corn Dryer, Struggs Hill, *Clare Best* 43
Trumpeters, *Henry Shukman* 44
Piano Man, *John Mole* 46
Billie Holliday at Carnegie Hall, *Linda France* 48
Lallation, *Gaia Holmes* 49
The City is a Drunk, *Mark Gwynne Jones* 50
A Second, *Hannah Silva* 52
Sonnet 128, *William Shakespeare* 53
Music: An Ode, *Algernon Charles Swinburne* 54
Cusp, *Roselle Angwin* 56
From River Sounding, *Mimi Khalvati* 57
Play, *David Hart* 58
Introduction Song of Innocence, *William Blake* 62
Questions for all Ages, *Chris Tutton* 63
Words for Music Perhaps, Girl's Song, *W B Yeats* 64
Words for Music Perhaps, Young Man's Song,
                                    W B Yeats 65

Concert, *Hannah Silva* 66
At Vondlepark, *Hannah Silva* 68
I am Lifting the Piano with One Hand, *Gaia Holmes* 69
At Lago Pilato, *Andrew Nightingale* 70
The Silence in the Garden, *Myra Schneider* 72

On Music, Thomas Moore   73

How Strange the Pain, Matt Harvey   74

The Wholesomeness of Coldplay and their Fans,
                                        Marvin Cheeseman   75

In the Light of This, Mark Gwynne Jones   76

Live Within This Music, Hannah Silva   78

Jig, Gaia Holmes   79

Blues for Bird, Linda France   80

To the Virgins, to Make Much of Time, Robert Herrick   82

lullaby without voices, Clare Best   83

A Musical Instrument, Elizabeth Barrett Browning   84

Mahler's Ninth, Myra Schneider   86

The End of Time, Mary MacRae   88

From Spring Days to Winter, Oscar Wilde   90

The Lake Isle of Innisfree, W B Yeats   91

Obit, Alison Brackenbury   92

The Woodcarver, Andrew Nightingale   93

The Fallow Yield, Chris Tutton   94

Summer Haiku, Leonard Cohen   97

On the Shoreline, Wendy French   98

The Cricket, Alison Brackenbury   99

Music, Walter de la Mare   100

Schuman at Midnight, Katrina Porteous   101

Like Casablanca, John Mole   102

Rain Bird, Nick Drake   103

Jerusalem, William Blake   104

The Fascinating Chill that Music Leaves,
                                        Emily Dickinson   105

Stanzas for Music, *Lord Byron   106*
April Sarabande, *Chris Tutton   107*
How Often Does It Happen, *Jane Draycott   108*
Near but Far Away, *William Morris   109*
Song for St Cecilia's Day, *John Dryden   110*
Twilight, *Rose Cook   113*
The Magic Flute, *Myra Schneider   114*
Skimming, *Anne Caldwell   116*
A Polar Carol, *John Mole   117*
Tarantella, *Hilaire Belloc   118*
question, *Clare Best   120*
Frank Sinatra Poem, *Marvin Cheeseman   121*
Wonder in the Nineties, *Andrew Nightingale   122*
Aerodrome, *Jane Draycott   124*
Rebetika, *Katrina Porteous   125*
Sonnet 8, *William Shakespeare   126*
In the Bleak Midwinter, *Christina Rossetti   127*
"Song though is a uniquely human experience",
*   Alison Brackenbury   128*
On the Aerial, *Alison Brackenbury   129*
If Love was Jazz, *Linda France   130*
Onward City Moments, *Matt Harvey   132*
Ode to a Pop Singer, *Chris Tutton   133*
Wild Garlic, *Mark Gwynne Jones   134*
On the Beach, *Roselle Angwin   136*
Lunar Eclipse, *Anne Caldwell   138*
At Remenham, *Jane Draycott   139*
Auld Laing Syne, *Robert Burns   140*

SYMPHONY

Thunder plays a piano
Piece for left hand
Cello storms after
Woodwind in a
Penguin suit sky
Moonlight intermezzo
Melts into first quiet
Chords of daybreak
Shimmering like
Young leaves on
Branches arced with rain.

Chris Tutton

THE SONG

I would write words
For the song you tried to teach me
Humming it in snatches
Saying *It goes something like this*
Which is all I can remember,
Since when your forgetfulness
Has been a gift as precious
As that summer afternoon,
Its long grass lying
Printed where we lay,
Our laughter a notation
Carrying on the breeze
In search of what might still
Return to us, reclaimed
And set to music
With such words as these

John Mole

PIANO SOLO

Years after my mother chose emptiness
at night high in my room I'd hear her
at the piano, planting chords, waiting
for them to grow into something.

She never advanced from childhood
lessons. She'd crackle flat a dry page
of Bartok or *Anna Magdalena*
and make the house's spine go cold.

That was all her hesitant handfuls
conjured – misery, a lonely beginner
always beginning again, a weather
of notes I wished would pass.

They trickled onto my sheets
in the dark, each drop telling
how sad a woman could feel
even to have lost what made her sad.

Henry Shukman

FROM RIVER SOUNDING

I have heard two voices in the river,
one of the singer, one of the listener
and both were the voices of poetry.

One was a daughter and one a son,
one would listen as the other ran on
and both could do either equally.

Where one was blind, the other was dumb,
when one of them wept, the other grew numb,
changing place simultaneously.

I have felt two terrors in my heart.
If one fell silent, the other would start
but it was the silent one that broke me.

Time stepped in to heal the breach
till both of my terrors were out of reach
and I returned to normality.

But the river ran on, I knew it was there
in the either/or, the when and where,
hiding, dividing, mercilessly.

Mimi Khalvati

MUSIC I HEARD

Music I heard with you was more than music,
And bread I broke with you was more than bread;
Now that I am without you, all is desolate;
All that was once so beautiful is dead.

Your hands once touched this table and this silver,
And I have seen your fingers hold this glass.
These things do not remember you, beloved,
And yet your touch upon them will not pass.

For it was in my heart that you moved among them,
And blessed them with your hands and with your eyes;
And in my heart they will remember always,
- They knew you once, O beautiful and wise.

Conrad Aiken

CELLO SUITES

i
Rostropovich, King's College Chapel

It was there, between us, palpable –
wrapped in blue air, outlined almost
in gold, like dust from the wings
of an angel (if such things existed),
damming the music in its flood
like a heavenly blood-clot, clenching
ventricles, nailing the heart
to the great ribbed vaulting (this landbound
ark) and one of us crying, it's not
clear who, as if for joy, or loss; and the dust
stirs briefly like the tremors of love
satisfied, or of grief. And it's gone

and you catch yourself thinking
this is the moment; this mystery,
this is where history starts.
And somewhere else a wing unfurls;
here, you're caught up once
and lifted, shipwrecked, drowning.

ii
Steven Isserlis, Exeter Cathedral

After all those words
a river of uncluttered notes.
'I'd like to be voiceless now
for days,' you whisper.

Something beyond language
opens its wings inside us;
bears us out streaming
into blue silence.

Roselle Angwin

FOOTPRINTS

I searched for metric meanings
along the grinding beach,
but despite my mystic leanings
they were always out of reach.

I dug for deeper answers
beneath the padded sands,
but all I found were dancers
with seaweed on their hands.

Though I boned up on the history
and strove to keep the score,
the sea remained a mystery
and I remained ashore.

Still I'd seek to know the essence
of what I am today,
for the proof of my pale presence
will soon be washed away,

and the seedbed of my questions
will be covered by the sea,
where my bones shall find a rest-home
when I'm no longer me.

Though I remember all the faces
and record what I have seen
the sea will wash away the traces
as though they'd never been.

For the sea's here to remind us
as we walk upon the land
that all we leave behind us
are footprints in the sand.

And footprints in the sand, it's said,
however deep and wide,
will not keep their distinctive tread
beyond the next high tide.

We pay ourselves such compliments
yet barely understand
the greatest of our monuments
are footprints in the sand.

Matt Harvey

PEARL

Not the pearl that murmurs
untroubled dreams of silk
and milkiness – that cool jewel
male poets once seized on
as a metaphor for teeth
or the loved one herself.

Not pearl, a smooth casing
the bi-sexual creature
makes to ease itself away
from sand grains and parasites
intruding between the lid
which hold it in a cool house.

Not the cased heart throbbing
as it pumps heat from room
to room, not the flames growing
behind the oven's glass door,
not even the intense
blue lick from filaments.

But the flesh within walls
that breathes, stirs, eats and makes –
the soft flesh so easily
stung, pecked or ripped apart.

Myra Schneider

THE ARTIST AT 81

Plain truth has become his only ornament,
Beguilement, first nature. With one white handkerchief
He will conjure the real world! Each hydra hand
Will meet the span required.

His repertoire goes down like a favourite meal:
His mind and heart savour the exact weight
Of all the notes, as one by one they ripen
Each in its own tempo.

It does not surprise him that the audience weeps:
Long ago, tears were the motherland
Of all his craft, twins to the blinding gems
Pinned to a tyrant's chest.

In this, his fine economy of age,
Nothing is show. Simply his music spells
A fluency of blessing to drown out
The worst of history. He need not even look
To know that we are weeping.

Lawrence Sail

ITALIAN MUSIC IN DAKOTA

["The Seventeenth – The finest Regimental Band I ever
heard."]

Through the soft evening air enwinding all,
Rocks, woods, fort, cannon, pacing sentries, endless wilds,
In dulcet streams, in flutes' and cornets' notes,
Electric, pensive, turbulent, artificial,
(Yet strangely fitting even here, meanings unknown before,
Subtler than ever, more harmony, as if born here, related here,
Not to the city's fresco'd rooms, not to the audience to the opera
house,
Sounds, echoes, wandering strains, as really here at home,
Sonnambula's innocent love, trios with Norma's anguish,
And thy ecstatic chorus Poliuto;)
Ray'd in the limpid yellow slanting sundown,

Music, Italian music in Dakota.
While Nature, sovereign of this gnarl'd realm,
Lurking in hidden barbaric grim recesses,
Acknowledging rapport however far remov'd,
(As some old root or soil of earth its last-born flower or fruit,)
Listens well pleas'd.

Walt Whitman

52nd STREET

The black cars are crackling like a wireless
in the rain, shining like the sweat

on a black man's cheeks as he plays
the trumpet sweeter than an angel. Neon

is hot as chilli, spiking your tongue,
tempting you in whichever joint

is jumping highest. It only costs
a dollar to step down into the cellar

where soon you'll be touching the sky. All
the shadows will be your friends. The music

fingers, plucks and blows the dark away –
brass, ivory, sycamore, skin – a glass

in your hand, a foot that won't stop tapping.

Linda France

THE 23.30 FROM LONDON

This, the sleepers' coach, purrs past the river,
the restaurants, the bridges' steel, the shimmer
of ring roads where a fox speeds out of sight.
We stumble off in small towns, Swindon, Worcester.

This is the sleepers' coach, but not tonight.
Our driver, from the country, old and bright,
free on the wide roads after days of ice
flicks on the music, whistles with delight,

swoops like a blackbird. But the station is
Called Magic, and its songs peel back my lives.
Here are guitars I listened to in bed,
breathing the smoke of coffee, warm with sex.

Here is the black singer, who demanded
justice and pity, whom my daughter heard
when we were richer, in a polished car,
later, as it rusted, with hearts battered.

Then new sounds soar and rush, for which I care
more urgently, since I cannot be here
for ever. What do their words give to me,
this world we made them? Anger, speed, and fear.

The coach has crossed an unseen boundary.
Magic has left the driver, rain and me.
I hurtle, from your party and good food,
into the song we shall not make, but be.

Alison Brackenbury

SCOTTISH BARONIAL

When I think of it now, it opens like a music box,
That dank castle overlooking the estuary.
Up an overgrown cart-track we found it at dusk,
Rooks in its narrow turrets, it slates awry.

There was talk of a benefits scam. A rag-bag
Assortment of travellers, skunk-dealers, tree-dwellers, healers
With crystals and feathers, holed up, burning candles
And sometimes the furniture, under its lofty ceilings.

And there was your daughter, pale, dreadlocked; and the first
                                                    of six
Dusty grand pianos; and one after another,
You threw those great rooms open, and every one
Flooded with music of a different colour;

Those poor, out-of-tune, rattling pianos –
Fin-de-siècle exiles of concert-hall or ball-room
Long fallen silent before the vanishing tide
Out on the mud-flats – singing, one last time.

Katrina Porteous

THE DAY IS DONE

The day is done, and the darkness
Falls from the wings of Night,
As a feather is wafted downward
From an eagle in his flight.

I see the lights of the village
Gleam through the rain and the mist,
And a feeling of sadness comes o'er me
That my soul cannot resist:

A feeling of sadness and longing,
That is not akin to pain,
And resembles sorrow only
As the mist resembles the rain.

Come, read to me some poem,
Some simple and heartfelt lay,
That shall soothe this restless feeling,
And banish the thoughts of day.

Not from the grand old masters,
Not from the bards sublime,
Whose distant footsteps echo
Through the corridors of Time.

For, like strains of martial music,
Their mighty thoughts suggest
Life's endless toil and endeavour,
And to-night I long for rest.

Read from some humbler poet,
Whose songs gushed from his heart,
As showers from the clouds of summer
Or tears from the eyelids start;

Who, through long days of labour,
And nights devoid of ease,
Still heard in his soul the music
Of wonderful melodies.

Such songs have power to quiet
The restless pulse of care,
And come like the benediction
That follows after prayer.

Then read from the treasured volume
The poem of thy choice,
And lend to the rhyme of the poet
The beauty of thy voice.

And the night shall be filled with music,
And the cares, that infest the day,
Shall fold their tents, like the Arabs,
And as silently steal away.

Henry Wadsworth Longfellow

SUNDAY MORNING -
CHICHESTER CLOISTERS

The ringers take a rest, biceps pulsing with heat
and the weight of the ropes. There's a lull,
full of that call to prayer to a god I no longer believe in.
The silence is bell-shaped and green.
I've time to contemplate millions of insects
in the oak spreading above my head:
pupating, living and dying in the shade.
A crow squawks. The bell ringers are ready.
Once lives were measured by chromatic scales
with a stumble in the middle, Now, my Sunday's
punctured by planes stacked up over Gatwick,
a ring-tone somewhere in my bag, car alarms
wailing for their owners, lines of metal bodies
rocking in the rush hour traffic.

Anne Caldwell

HEART WE WILL FORGET HIM

Heart, we will forget him!
You and I, tonight!
You may forget the warmth he gave,
I will forget the light.

When you have done, pray tell me
That I my thoughts may dim;
Haste! lest while you're lagging.
I may remember him!

Emily Dickinson

WRITING TO SOMEONE ELSE'S MUSIC

I predict my own. It opens between notes. It licks. It licks. It likes the sound in a cell. The piano next door, everyone flees. In a derelict momentum we travel across bridges. A serpent and another empty house. An inside out. The belongings reveal. They reveal a body working in spite of itself. A fake sun on leaves. How did we leave these flakes of ourselves so visible? So visible.

Wanting is this air thinking. Sun on sun on now now no. I touch breasts. They milk smooth in the cupping. Nipples pink nipples drown dribble ripple down own. To kill this body with skin I run.

Look at him run. He is sweat thigh as dust cries. Look at his eyes. Cry their found look. His eyes look found. In his tears his running   beats.   What   about   your   music? The streets fall behind and and

What are you doing? Why are you here? What's that noise? I'm walking towards you. I've been here since yesterday. This is my perfect. My perfect kindness. Have me.

You looked different yesterday. My shiver on a dream. Playing on a grand piano while the disintegration surrounds. Will the torn sound repent? All the tears touch each other. They like to be touched. This is someone else's disease. Shared she he here, descend end end

tktktktktktktktktktktktk too long taking too long taking looking what do you think about this bit?

Ah oo looking a ee, are you ooee at I mouth? And wantee ah oo
are standing so eee still that I ao know I know no one one

This, watched I. Until it, down the last page walked. It took the
hand, and in hand in. Look at the dust. Look how smooth the
mark is left. Look how the traces match the waiting costs. I
think this is like whispering to friends who listen tight. The
sounds at night seem to echo this thought. Like an emptiness.

Hannah Silva

FORGETFULNESS

We awake:
dog-eared, moth-bitten,
noctilucent clouds
still colouring
our blood.
Last night
we forgot things.
A man danced,
spoke in tongues
for his past,
babbled
something like love
and we sang
for his dance,
we sang with smoke,
with fire,
with forgetfulness.
We sang dry throated
and dreaming
through the witching hour..
Now, in the morning
our tongues smolder
like the ashes
where we burnt
our little demons
on tiny slips of light

Gaia Holmes

A SERENADE AT THE VIILA

That was I, you heard last night,
Where there rose no moon at all,
Nor, to pierce the strained and tight
Tent of heaven, a planet small:
Life was dead and so was light.

Not a twinkle from the fly,
Not a glimmer from the worm;
When the crickets stopped their cry,
When the owls forbore a term,
You heard music; that was I.

Earth turned in her sleep with pain,
Sultrily suspired for proof:
In at heaven and out again,
Lightning!---where it broke the roof,
Bloodlike, some few drops of rain.

What they could my words expressed,
O my love, my all, my one!
Singing helped the verses best,
And when singing's bcst was donc,
To my lute I left the rest.

So wore night; the East was grey,
White the broad-faced hemlock-flowers:
There would be another day;
Ere its first of heavy hours
Found me, I had passed away.

What became of all the hopes,
Words and song and lute as well?
Say, this struck you---"when life gropes
  Feebly for the path where fell
  Light last on the evening slopes,

One friend in that path shall be,
To secure my step from wrong;
One to count night day for me,
Patient through the watches long,
Serving most with none to see."

Never say---as something bodes---
  "So, the worst has yet a worse!
When life halts 'neath double loads,
Better the taskmaster's curse
Than such music on the roads!

When no moon succeeds the sun,
Nor can pierce the midnight's tent
Any star, the smallest one,
While some drops, where lightning rent,
Show the final storm begun---

When the fire-fly hides its spot,
When the garden voices fail
In the darkness thick and hot,---
Shall another voice avail,
That shape be where these are not?

Has some plague a longer lease,
Proffering its help uncouth?
Can't one even die in peace?
As one shuts one's eyes on youth,
Is that face the last one sees?"

Oh how dark your villa was,
Windows fast and obdurate!
How the garden grudged me grass
Where I stood---the iron gate
Ground its teeth to let me pass!

Robert Browning

NICO
(age 10)

I have your language but will not speak it,
not to you, not least because you think
you own it and would make it mine.
Each word I learn must enter by permission
at a gate marked Private. We conspire
to keep you out. You ask how it is
you deserved this. Ask the words, not me.
Maybe they fear correction, maybe
but I doubt it. The more of them there are
the more they tell me language is power
and that I have it, that silence is golden
only when, like mine, it's a promise
to be withdrawn, a gift I have to offer
or choose not to accept. They tell me
there's no telling what you would have me do
if the gate fell open and I let you in,
and so I keep it locked. The password
changes as each day they give me
more to guard. Together we evade
your inquisition of control, we understand
that it is kindly meant and meet it
with a pale smile and my furtive shrug
of casual shoulders. Somewhere
between love and patience, puzzlement
and fear, the answer I withhold
may greet its question, maybe so,
but word by word, and certainly for now,
I own a secret that is mine to keep.

John Mole

LOSING THE LANGUAGE

I roll words I remember like gobstoppers of pure sugar,
or amber beads, each with a trapped creature
longing to flex its wings.

I've a kirk and a kirk-yaird, a herring quine's empty kist,
flooer-beds of roses gardening the streets
of Airberdeen. I've a view of the driech sea

from an auld hoose, a winda in a tooer block.
I've one snap of my faither when he was a bairn
in a cowboy suit. That's about the sum of it.

At night, I listen for the murmur of the Caledonian Sleeper,
loop beads about my throat and wear silk.
Upstairs; my red-haired child is freckled with dreams.

Anne Caldwell

STENTOR HYWEL

My first real taste of yr hen iaith fy nhadau:
Bulbous browed and sweatily unkempt
He'd utter cynghaneddau with an imprecator's zeal,
Relishing our flaccid sais responses.

I hear now, Hywel, you have lost your voice
And sit glazed in a care home chair;
Heb os nac oni bai
An undeserved turn
Your broken back of language.

Lawrence Mathias

THERE CAME A WIND LIKE A BUGLE

There came a Wind like a Bugle -
It quivered through the Grass
And a Green Chill upon the Heat
So ominous did pass
We barred the Windows and the Doors
As from an Emerald Ghost -
The Doom's electric Moccasin
The very instant passed -
On a strange Mob of panting Trees
And Fences fled away
And Rivers where the Houses ran
Those looked that lived - that Day -
The Bell within the steeple wild
The flying tidings told -
How much can come
And much can go,
And yet abide the world!

Emily Dickinson

DRESS AND WAIT

Last time I saw you
you were standing on your own
in the moonlight,
outside a broken window
in an alley with a burned-out sign.
Your story was written all over your face
like lavatory wall graffiti;
now you live in another place
but the old men, they still
call you sweetie.

Now and then you feel like when
you used to dress for dates;
now and then you only
dress and wait.
Now and then you only
dress and wait.

In your paternoster bar-rooms,
in your sanctuary of drunken dreaming
you pay your piper well 'n so you
call the tunes you still believe in;
you run to keep from standing still
but still you stand to keep from drowning,
and you curse the ghost of morning,
'cos the dead of night just won't lie down.

Now and then you feel like when
you used to dress for dates;
now and then you only

dress and wait.
Now and then you only
dress and wait.

At the station you're still standing
with a suitcase in your hand
(ain't got a ticket),
you're smoking cigarettes and stuff
and say one day you're gonna kick it. And
in the limelight nyctophobic shadows you still
plant your kisses
on slick and sly then wave goodbye
and bid them all your fondest wishes....

Now and then you feel like when
you used to dress for dates;
now and then you only
dress and wait.
Now and then you only
dress and wait.

Chris Tutton

LEFT

They never sang to me.
Since they no longer stride the hill
or peg out creaking washing
they never will.

Grandmother's mother's desk
from the legendary lost farm
was salvaged by my parents
from dog food, sheep salves, grime.

They found, stuffed in the deep drawers,
penny notebooks. Letters were
traced airily, as spider-thin
as young Victoria.

Until a dashing black hand:
for sheep thrush, baby scour,
horse worming balls, from fenugreek
saltpetre, elderflower.

What's this? "I am a lady bright,
my love has listed, gone.
What care I for world or treasure?"
It is a song

which I will sing, flat, softly,
to great moon's glow, cold week.
The next page lists the lambs lost,
white sulphur, fenugreek.

Alison Brackenbury

CORN DRYER, STRUGGS HILL

We go there to witness silence, the grain all in,
but you need to tell me what I didn't see –
how the big wheels rumbled across the yard,
how this roof seemed to hover above the store
while wheat fields, peas and barley were heaped,
filling the silos like cereal bowls.
You want me to hear the whistles and shouts,
the makeshift percussion of conveyor belts.
You flick switches: engines shuffle and jerk;
acres of grain rattle over wire. When you know
I know, you turn off the machines.
Silence. Dust settling on shoulders and hair.

Clare Best

TRUMPETERS

Dad keeps his old trumpet in the cupboard.
The frayed leather case smells of dust.
The clips clunk, he lifts the lid. Inside,
the gold bell rests on its bed of velvet.
He wipes the gleaming tubes, sluices oil
in the valves, flicks them wheezing
on their springs. Tries a bar of *Ain't Misbehavin'*.

Humphrey did that. He peers at me over the bell.
Played with him once. Years ago, of course.
He can't help smiling as his cheeks inflate.
Play along, boychick, we're in C. I don't know
what to do, blow a bottom C on my rented
Boosey, then a G, while he splits his tune.
Better use the mutes, Helen's downstairs.

Rain plays a light snare on the skylight, leaves
stick to the glass, beyond them the sky is purple,
dark already at five. Out come the music cards,
the Salvation Army lyres with little brass screws.
We attempt *Away in a Manger, Once in Royal*.
In three weeks we'll be out, he and I, a carol duet
buttoned in our coats under a street lamp, fingers freezing.

I'll pay you to go away, a neighbour will cry,
half-joking. Dad will laugh into his instrument,
making it screech. For now in the yellow light
of his desk lamp we settle *While Shepherds Watched*

44

in the clips, press our lips against the mouthpieces,
against our muted harmony, as long as we can,
until downstairs calls and we put the trumpets away.

Henry Shukman

PIANO MAN
Oscar Peterson, Montreux 1974

Heavyweight but handy
With the glissandi,
On a held chord he lingers
Until the spread of those fingers
Contracts to a thumb
And he starts his run.

From a counterpoint fugue he
Breaks into boogie
And torrential sweat
But you ain't heard nothing yet.
Now suddenly gentle,
Blue and sentimental.

Athlete of jazz,
His racy razzmatazz
From hot to cool
Breaks every rule
But he knows that his act is
Perfected by practice.

The audience roars
And he rides its applause
To the finishing line
Then, taking his time,
He gets up to bow
And he wipes his brow.

Passion, skill, wit -
This has been it,
The perfect balance
Of thought and chance,
Jazz with a grin,
Spaced out, reined in.

And so he stands,
Those miraculous hands
Joined together there
As if in prayer
But now what they do
Is say Thank you. Thank you!

John Mole

BILLIE HOLIDAY AT CARNEGIE HALL

Her fingers mistook her hair
for a thought they had once
and let go and kept letting go
until the pin sunk into skin
tight on her scalp. Everyone

knows how much heads bleed.
Billie's black dress hid the stains.
Her three gardenias pouted,
white against the darkening red.
On stage, she held up her head

like she always did and sang
and kept on singing until the smell
had died the same way day falls
into night; its ghost cradling her,
that sweet motherish scent.

Linda France

LALLATION

Those nights of inhabiting
someone else's stories
have been locked away.
Stained cotton sheets
have been folded
and stacked in storage.
Dog-eared sprigs
of browned silk flowers
have been binned.
She has developed a cleaner,
more sophisticated technique
that uses the shaping of the mouth,
the pressure of the tongue
pushed against the teeth,
the soft delivery
of exquisite plosives
and shimmering fricatives,
the whisper of affricates
or the richer, darker songs
of Os and Es and As
swooping from her lips
like pipistrelles,
so that where once
there were distended eyes
and needling fingers
there is the calm burr
and cadence of her breath,
the erotic lallation
of her song.

Gaia Holmes

THE CITY IS A DRUNK

I saw him once,
laughing till he cried for his bastard dad.
  It was happy hour!
And with bags tied on his feet
he was laughing like a turnstile
spitting people on the street.
Laughing, at the gateway
to the underground.

Yes, the city is a drunk.

And he could talk for England
rambling like he does
from the station of Waterloo
to Elgar and the Wind
rush.
Rattling
        to the undertones
        of a diesel engine.
Coughing up the black soot
to sing like a sparrow
of fog and fumes and the time when he
was cock
        of the world.

Yes, the city is a drunk,
        harbouring hurt.
A secret kept on the north bank
in brambles. A tryst
where the devil hides in a brown shoe

and a shrine is made
of lady's basque, pearls and fur
gathered as if by a butcher bird
and decked with shards of coloured glass.
The gesture of a lonely man,
on bended knees where the nettles sting
and something there's reminding him
of country girls
long ago.

I saw him once
hands down the back of an old settee.
Red eye Joey Blakes
searching for something to stop the shakes
searching for something lost...

And who'd believe his promises,
who'd believe his
I could make you famous
        whispered over gin?
The pimp for a billion wannabes,
who'd believe in him?
Each place I go, only the lonely go...
In a moment he could change the world
                Some little small cafe
join up all the dots
                Think of the possibilities!...
groping the arse of an old settee
and leaving her undone.

Mark Gwynne Jones

51

A SECOND

rises and dissipates word
for emotion throat sudden
goes a word for emotion rises
sudden welling goes and

dissipates. A second should
be a word that rises and
disappears a sudden wailing
through the throat emotion for a word
wilting in a second

throat should appear dissipate
in a sudden veiling should a word
rising in motion and the word is patient
or hidden in a word for the notion
should be suddenly paled.

Is there a word for emotion
that rises for a second
and dissipates? A sudden
welling in the throat and it goes.

Hannah Silva

SONNET 128

How oft, when thou, my music, music play'st,
Upon that blessed wood whose motion sounds
With thy sweet fingers, when thou gently sway'st
The wiry concord that mine ear confounds,
Do I envy those jacks that nimble leap
To kiss the tender inward of thy hand,
Whilst my poor lips, which should that harvest reap,
At the wood's boldness by thee blushing stand!
To be so tickled, they would change their state
And situation with those dancing chips,
O'er whom thy fingers walk with gentle gait,
Making dead wood more blest than living lips.
Since saucy jacks so happy are in this,
Give them thy fingers, me thy lips to kiss.

William Shakespeare

MUSIC: AN ODE

Was it light that spake from the darkness,
or music that shone from the word,
When the night was enkindled with sound
of the sun or the first-born bird?
Souls enthralled and entrammelled in bondage
of seasons that fall and rise,
Bound fast round with the fetters of flesh,
and blinded with light that dies.
Lived not surely till music spake,
and the spirit of life was heard.
Music, sister of sunrise, and herald of life to be,
Smiled as dawn on the spirit of man,
and the thrall was free.
Slave of nature and serf of time,
the bondman of life and death,
Dumb with passionless patience that breathed
but forlorn and reluctant breath,
Heard, beheld, and his soul made answer,
and commuted aloud with the sea.

Morning spake, and he heard:
and the passionate silent noon
Kept for him not silence:
and soft from the mounting moon
Fell the sound of her splendour,
heard as dawn's in the breathless night,

Not of men but of birds whose note
bade man's soul quicken and leap to light:
And the song of it spake, and the light and the darkness
of earth were as chords in tune.

Algernon Charles Swinburne

CUSP

The wave's apex; that moment when it is poised
like a horse for the leap, and the sea's
haunches under it; when it is clean
as glass, unbroken; a silence sculpted from the surf's noise -

that moment; or another - that gone-in-a-flash
cusp between the you of here, now
putting the kettle on, or maybe that slow
piano passage; and then without really knowing it catching

an unguarded question in his eyes, and then both of you gone
tumbling over the lip, a cascade
from which emergence is not possible until too late
if at all; and the myth of return

merely a shadow between two cast-off lives;
beat, heartstop, between systole and diastole glimpsed
                                        and recognised.

Roselle Angwin

FROM RIVER SOUNDING

Without my love, there is no song.
Without my love, no silence.
A carousel without a pole,
two apple halves without a whole,
no centre, no circumference.

Without him, the idea of him,
desire draws up its blanket.
Stars come out and look about,
a halfway moon gives way to doubt
with no one here to thank it.

Ears grow deaf, eyes grow dim,
and why is the street so long?
The best is over, you know it is,
for he took your best and made it his
inimitable song.

Without my love, there is no song, etc.

Mimi Khalvati

PLAY

1
I thought, if I arrange the musical instruments
in order in the field
the angels will come and play them,

and the angels did come and they
kicked the instruments and trod them
into the ground,

and they threw the instruments
into the bog, and they snapped the instruments
in pieces as if they were branches for a fire,

and the fire almost woke me,
almost brought me back
to begin again.

2
I am an old man calling on a Dog Daisy
that will sing me its names: Oxeye, Marguerite, Moon,
and I shall say *Cure my eyes,* and it will say
   Duet with me
   greedily.

Cure my wounds, I say to Self-heal, on my knees.
So you have the quinsy?
It's not my throat palls, it's something else, soul's ills.
So jump up, dance!

The clouds have passed and I tell Silverweed

it can wake now, it can open wide, *Goosewort, I say,*
and by any other name you have, warn me.
And I do a goosey-goosey snap at it - it's a tease.
It opens with deep gaunt eyes and pauses and says,
Are you hungry? Eat me. My roots, roast them.

I beg of the Milk Thistle, who is Mary Thistle who is
Wild Artichoke, Blessed Milk Thistle, Marian, who is
St. Mary's Thistle, who is Lady Thistle, Holy,

and I make a joke I can't properly remember where
the liver says heal my man's soul, or the soul says
it's my liver, my liver,
>   and I lie down on my back
>   on the grass to live
>   for ever.

3
I thought, I will do the work of angels,
I will hold the pen, they will do the work,
and they came and stood around
and when I most wanted to hear clearly they
told loud obscene jokes and spoke in whispers,
and they ran around in circles
making fun of me. I stood my shaking ground,
the pen ready in my hand.
>   I thought,
if I am ready, they will do the rest,
I told myself this and if I didn't believe it
whose fault was that? I gave the angels so readily
their opportunity, I waited with my pen ready,
and they laughed at me, they kicked dust
that looked like words

into my notebook. I was, I knew then,
their plaything. A song was all I'd wanted,
the angels have so many, they could have (look at me)
spared me one, I waited with obvious longing, my pen
and my voice ready, I thought readiness
(what it really means as best intent, as best intent)
was what they wanted of me.

4

I can pretend a *squawk* but I can't fly,
I can say *swoosh swoosh* but I am not the sea,
I can say *baaaa* but I am not a sheep,

all day and night my not being other than I am
in this quiet place is accompanied by waves
and gulls and sheep and wind under the door,

no-one is playing music on the island
and the island is awash with sounds,
coming off the rocks closer inshore the seals.

Through the sedge a grass-snake attends me
as whisper, a clout of a cloud comes over and
on to the outcrop pelts out rain like a clatter

of dropped nails, back in the hut a mouse is
racing around all the walls making a sound
like a child playing at sweeping, a large bee

is hitting the window like a jazz blues drummer.
This is a day's music in high summer here.

5

So I thought, if the angels would like my life
they would have to wrench it from me, I would
put up an absurd fight, on my knees
I would wrestle them off. What to say on such a day
to represent intention, urgency, foolishness?

6

Almost midnight and with Byrd's Four Part Mass
I enter into the dark *in excelsis,* then the Five-Part,
laudamus te, now the Three-Part, *dona nobis pacem,* now
again the Four-Part *eleison, eleison, eleison,* and on
again and again
                              into the night.

David Hart

SONGS OF INNOCENCE
INTRODUCTION

Piping down the valleys wild,
Piping songs of pleasant glee,
On a cloud I saw a child,
And he laughing said to me:

"Pipe a song about a lamb!"
So I piped with merry cheer.
"Piper, pipe that song again,"
So I piped: he wept to hear.

"Drop thy pipe, thy happy pipe;
Sing thy songs of happy cheer!"
So I sung the same again,
While he wept with joy to hear.

"Piper, sit thee down and write
In a book, that all may read."
So he vanished from my sight,

And I plucked a hollow reed,
And I made a rural pen,
And I stained the water clear,
And I wrote my happy songs
Every child may joy to hear.

William Blake

QUESTIONS FOR ALL AGES

We wished our
Fragile voices
Could be
Drowned in song
As we
Patiently waited
For all nine choirs
To break their silence.

Chris Tutton

FROM WORDS FOR MUSIC PERHAPS
GIRL'S SONG

I went out alone
To sing a song or two,
My fancy on a man,
And you know who.
Another came in sight
That on a stick relied
To hold himself upright;
I sat and cried.
And that was all my song – –
When everything is told,
Saw I an old man young
Or young man old?

W B Yeats

FROM WORDS FOR MUSIC PERHAPS
YOUNG MAN'S SONG

'She will change,' I cried.
'Into a withered crone.'
The heart in my side,
That so still had lain,
In noble rage replied
And beat upon the bone:
'Uplift those eyes and throw
Those glances unafraid:
She would as bravely show
Did all the fabric fade;
No withered crone I saw
Before the world was made.'
Abashed by that report,
For the heart cannot lie,
I knelt in the dirt.
And all shall bend the knee
To my offended heart
Until it pardon me.

W B Yeats

1. CONCERT

The concert happens at the top of a flat
on an Amsterdam street.

There is a skylight and the room is hot.

You've been refused music.
He took away half your instrument,

gave back a simple mouthpiece.
You can't do anything with it.

Want to scream.
Should have been a cellist.

Want to kick the baroque era
up the arse, become romantic.

But when you hold the
mouthpiece, that wooden

blokflute between your lips a sound
escapes: a harmonic.

Octaves above
any music you'd thought of.

It's a sound trapped in the middle of a
sound; barely a gasp.

You practice it. Over and over.
Hours, a gasp and a skylight.

Hannah Silva

2. VONDLEPARK

When morning arrives there's an absence
in her stomach, her breath has escaped.

She trips down stairs, cycles
through the Vondlepark, looks for green
parrots. Can't help smiling at the drunk
with rotten teeth who yesterday said:

I want to kiss you all over.

The note follows.
She presents it to her teacher.

There's something beneath that sound.

She is confused.
He explains:

The strange noise that escaped as you were about to play.

She tries to repeat it.
She can't.

He tells her to go away and practice some more.

Hannah Silva

I AM LIFTING THE PIANO WITH ONE HAND

I am holding it effortlessly steady
like a gliding waiter balancing a tray
of quail's eggs and salmon souffle
on his horizantal palm.

I am dexterously carrying it up three flights of stairs
without stubbing my toes or splitting my fingernails,
without chipping paint off the door frames
or denting the soft plaster of the walls.

I am lifting the piano with one hand.
I have not eaten spinach, mineral supplements,
muscle powder or Weetabix.
Today I am just incredibly strong
and able to carry the piano up three flights of stairs
where I'll leave the skylight window open

and a note inviting any passing ghosts
to come in, sit down and play 'Moonlight Sonata'
or 'Chopin's Nocturne' or 'The Entertainer'
or whatever they'd like to play on a neglected piano
in the house of a very strong woman.

Gaia Holmes

AT LAGO PILATO

Each footfall on the climb compacts
shattered bones of limestone
that chink in the tinny air until
a brook cuts across our way –
we pause to dip our hands,
scooping liquid prisms to our brows.
Then the shimmering path entreats
our pondrous inching steps again.

At six thousand feet, the glacial valley
comes to rest in a malevolent lake:
two fused bulbs of black water
fed on a slick of crackling snow.
A ring of glowering buttresses keeps
the water dammed in a bowl of scree,
lifted up, an offering to the thin sky.

Hello – lo – lo – hello – lo

The cry gutters on slurred perspective.

You try

The dizzying roar of ecstatic rock face
seems to rush forward then suddenly recede.
The bleary light is sparse, gulped.
I can't think anymore.

In the gap I leave, again you call

Hello – lo – lo – ello

Dull, aching repetitions,
canons of numbness tested
against blanks of ice, withering scarps.
Your call searches the monotone valley,
only to find itself again –
the conquering voice, swirling
into its own heady answer and dying.

Andrew Nightingale

71

THE SILENCE IN THE GARDEN

No rule forbids speech but no one's talking. Quiet
grows from dark densities between boughs,
from heart-shaped leaves covering the ground,
their tight creamwhite umbrellas, flows

from spheres, spirals, hollows, undulations.
We come upon a hooded figure, trace spaces
that so poignantly speak her body. With hands
in a scoop that's river, wordlessly we unlace

the emerald hair of splayed weeds, silts
where fleshy roots bed, black threads
squirming from eggs. We don't need to name
the moment when twined swirls of bronze read

as petals unfolding outwards – corollas
frail as small birds' wings and as strong –
or the moment when a surge beneath the lid
makes the box of possibility spring

open. As if placing shoes outside a temple
we left our voices in the street by the gate,
entered another language. And now, sitting
by the untroubled waters, we dip feet.

Myra Schneider

Barbara Hepworth's garden, St Ives

ON MUSIC

When thro' life unblest we rove,
Losing all that made life dear,
Should some notes we us'd to love,
In days of boyhood, meet our ear,
Oh! how welcome breathes the strain!
Wakening thoughts that long have slept!
Kindling former smiles again
In faded eyes that long have wept.

Like the gale, that sighs along
Beds of oriental flowers,
Is the grateful breath of song,
That once was heard in happier hours;
Fill'd with balm, the gale sighs on,
Though the flowers have sunk in death;
So, when pleasure's dream is gone,
Its memory lives in Music's breath.

Music! oh how faint, how weak,
Language fades before thy spell!
Why should Feeling ever speak,
When thou canst breathe her soul so well?
Friendship's balmy words may feign,
Love's are ev'n more false than they;
Oh! tis only Music's strain
Can sweetly soothe, and not betray!

Thomas Moore

HOW STRANGE THE PAIN

How strange the pain
that comes again
when I had thought it gone

And that bright ray
that shone today
diverts itself another's way
when I had thought it here to stay
to be relied upon

How quaint the ache
that seeks to break
a body's very heart

The pop song sings
of the strain it brings
and milks the tears with glissando strings
and half-choked sobs and sighs and things
to pull it wide apart

And make some room
in the grief-grey gloom
for a sense both old and new

A sense of grace
in a cold, dark place
that lends the strength to turn and face
the inbred fear of the empty space
that needs attending to

Matt Harvey

74

THE WHOLESOMENESS OF COLDPLAY AND THEIR FANS

Lines written at Old Trafford in late summer 2009

A squeaky-clean affair indeed
Not a trace of crack or weed
Coldplay fans formed ordered queues
For t-shirts, programmes, pies and booze
Prim and proper, well behaved
Nothing vulgar, or depraved
Just well-heeled, well-scrubbed punters where
Not one foul word defiled the air
No low-life scum to lower the tone
Not one pint pot of piss got thrown
Not one theft, not one arrest
Cliff Richard would have been impressed
Chris Martin, arms outstretched, divine
My bottled water turned to wine
This saintly chap sang one last song
The congregation sang along...

...Then left, blessed, cleansed and holier

To gently paint the town magnolia.

Marvin Cheeseman

IN THE LIGHT OF THIS

the moon is dim
and the sun is but a ball
of hydrogen: a chemical formula
set on fire

by the light of this

people draw
daydreams on the bathroom wall
a picture of you opening the fridge
dressed only

in the light of this

lovers meet
beneath the clock above the street
and sharing secrets they become
as one

in the light of this

we catch a glimpse
of the force that makes the world to spin
and your eyes shine
like the night shines

in the light of this

you can read
my thoughts and tell me what they mean

or slap me hard across the face
say: *Come round...half-past-eight...*
bring some wine and don't be late...

then in the dark we'll explore
places that we've been before
but never really understood

by the light of this

Mark Gwynne Jones

LIVE WITHIN THIS MUSIC

from which the out is observed and closed
held close
and served

taken the metres and danced within them have we
counted the beats
barred the lines we
have within them danced and
held close
and closed

as sure as
undo awe
undo or
you're sure
essence
as usual
sensitively
still life still alive
we wear these senses unusually

Hannah Silva

JIG

there is
the smoke

and the scratch
and the jig

of bones
and the wheeze

of leaves
and the spark

in the eye
and the bellows

flaming
the flailing heart

and a magician stands
in my front room

bringing
my dead words
back to life

Gaia Holmes

BLUES FOR BIRD

What you did to the blues
was the sound of a bird
trapped behind broken glass
beating at the liquid
light, struggling to fly free.
You crushed bones with your horn.

They all told you a horn
shouldn't be blown that free
and fast. You played the blues
hot as neon, liquid
gas. Your sax and a glass
of booze – you were a bird.

And they called you *Yard bird*
too, singing back home blues
twitching that brassy horn
full of amber liquid –
those notes that shone like glass
made you dream you were free.

Say who of us is free?
We all live under glass
wishing we were bird,
sky gold with angel horn.
But we swim in the blues –
indigo, turquoise, liquid

as the sea. Your liquid
cocktail was spiked with horn
of horse. Nothing is free.
On the streets, doing bird
they followed you, those blues –
tears just mirrors of glass.

But still you'd fill your glass,
pick up, polish your horn.
The tune spilled like liquid
from your lips. You were free
as death – your soul a bird.
You earned your breath, your blues.

Bird, you're a ghost of glass,
liquid mid all those blues –
free at last, your horn, you.

Linda France

TO THE VIRGINS, TO MAKE MUCH OF TIME

Gather ye rosebuds while ye may
Old time is still a-flying:
And this same flower that smiles today
Tomorrow will be dying.

The glorious lamp of heaven, the sun,
The higher he's a-getting,
The sooner will his race be run,
And nearer he's to setting.

That age is best which is the first,
When youth and blood are warmer;
But being spent, the worse, and worst
Times still succeed the former.

Then be not coy, but use your time,
And while ye may go marry:
For having lost but once your prime
You may for ever tarry.

Robert Herrick

lullaby without voices

he's with them still
        the one who wasn't born
with them in the night

waking to a bright half-moon
        sky and clouds
all shades of blue and grey

they're sure he's with them
        still the little one
who had no time

shifting   dark
        between them
a phantom in their boat

Clare Best

A MUSICAL INSTRUMENT

What was he doing, the great god Pan,
Down in the reeds by the river?
Spreading ruin and scattering ban,
Splashing and paddling with the hoofs of a goat,
And breaking the golden lilies afloat
With the dragon-fly on the river.

He tore out a reed, the great god Pan,
From the deep cool bed of the river.
The limpid water turbidly ran,
And the broken lilies a-dying lay,
And the dragon-fly had fled away,
Ere he brought it out of the river.

High on the shore sat the great god Pan
While turbidly flowed the river;
And hacked and hewed as a great god can,
With his hard bleak steel at the patient reed,
Till there was not a sign of the leaf indeed
To prove it fresh from the river.

He cut it short, did the great god Pan,
(How tall it stood in the river!)
Then drew the pith, like the heart of a man,
Steadily from the outside ring,
And noticed the poor dry empty thing
In holes, as he sat by the river.

'This is the way,' laughed the great god Pan
(Laughed while he sat by the river),
'The only way, since gods began
To make sweet music, they could succeed.'
Then, dropping his mouth to a hole in the reed,
He blew in power by the river.

Sweet, sweet, sweet, O Pan!
Piercing sweet by the river!
Blinding sweet, O great god Pan!
The sun on the hill forgot to die,
And the lilies revived, and the dragon-fly
Came back to dream on the river.

Yet half a beast is the great god Pan,
To laugh as he sits by the river,
Making a poet out of a man:
The true gods sigh for the cost and pain, --
For the reed which grows nevermore again
As a reed with the reeds in the river.

Elizabeth Barrett Browning

MAHLER'S NINTH

for Mary MacRae

No music in Le Pain Quotidien. Voices clatter,
crockery shrills white but the raspberries in my tartlet
are unblemished, lucent as the red in your poem.

'If it wasn't for the noise this would be perfect,'
I say, 'but we can't have everything.'
And at once I see you, my dear friend,

in a coma in hospital three miles away –
you can't have anything. You're in my head
as we join the pilgrims trailing down Exhibition Road.

In the Albert Hall we all wait for the symphony
Mahler composed when he learnt he had an illness
doctors couldn't cure, the symphony he never heard.

Its beginning is tentative as if the instruments
are trying to find a way to talk to one another.
Phrases quiver into findings which become losings

but as the movement closes harmony's found.
Now, somewhere in the surge of strings, poignancy
of woodwind is you, Mary, and 'the brightness of red'

you 'want to be inside.' Too soon we arrive
at the finale. The music opens out, soars
but each time it nears a climax it retreats.

How will this end – with orchestra and audience
lifting to those waterlily circles spanning
the dome? No, the instruments are quietening,

their hushed voices hover, slip away.
There isn't anything now but the five thousand
held together in a silence larger than sound.

Myra Schneider

THE END OF TIME

On this bitter January night
sometime after six o'clock, with snow
blowing under the barrack door

in Stalag VIIIA, rows of prisoners,
skeletons hung with rags
against the Silesian winter,

listen – for an hour, for their lives –
to what no-one has ever heard before.
What hunger for it in the men listening,

the blue-orange chords on the keyboard
falling weightless, the colours of sunrise,
and each new cadence sounding like home.

How many gathered there – five hundred,
five thousand? No-one remembers.
Whatever the number, all still

as if an angel crowned with a rainbow
had come and sounded the trumpet
as a sign that time has ended.

Wearing clogs, playing a broken piano
the composer asks the impossible:
the clarinettist must hold his note

until he leaves earth behind, the cellist
move his bow so inhumanly slowly
he reaches towards silence.

They feel their way through pathless rhythms.
'Never', Messiaen says, 'have I been listened to
with such attention, such understanding.'

Mary MacRae

FROM SPRING DAYS TO WINTER (FOR MUSIC)

In the glad sprintime when leaves were green,
O merrily the thostle sings!
I sought, amid the tangled sheen,
Love whom mine eyes had never seen,
O the glad dove has golden wings!

Between the blossoms red and white,
O merrily the thostle sings!
My love first came into my sight,
O perfect vision of delight,
O the glad dove has golden wings!

The yellow apples glowed like fire,
O merrily the thostle sings!
O Love too great for lip or lyre,
Blown rose of love and of desire,
O the glad dove has golden wings!

But now with snow the tree is grey,
Ah, sadly now the thostle sings!
My love is dead: ah! well-a-day,
See at her silent feet I lay
A dove with broken wings!
Ah, Love! ah, Love! that thou wert slain –
Fond Dove, fond Dove return again!

Oscar Wilde

THE LAKE ISLE OF INNISFREE

I will arise and go now, and go to Innisfree,
And a small cabin build there, of clay and wattles made;
Nine bean rows will I have there, a hive for the honeybee,
And live alone in the bee-loud glade.

And I shall have some peace there, for peace comes dropping
                                                    slow,
Dropping from the veils of the morning to where the cricket
                                                    sings;
There midnight's all a-glimmer, and noon a purple glow,
And evening full of the linnet's wings.

I will arise and go now, for always night and day
I hear lake water lapping with low sounds by the shore;
While I stand on the roadway, or on the pavements grey,
I hear it in the deep heart's core.

W B Yeats

OBIT

This is for them, wide-eyed or drunk or mad
who called me "Angela", who played by ear,
who did not stay, robust, in my dull life,
but fell before the dark time of the year.
I wished I had laughed longer at their jokes,
twanged mandolins, been brave. But I am here.
My lesson done, beside the light's cracked door
I play all love dictates for them, by ear.

Alison Brackenbury

THE WOODCARVER

An old man is sitting by the Rialto.
He whittles at a figurine,
intricate fingers searching
for the human form
in the gnarl and knot of the seasons.

Each figurine becomes a languid adolescent,
a stretched uncluttered chord
placed once and left to sound
on a grand piano.

He died on a February night,
his stiff body propped on frosty cobbles.
They handled him like antique wood,
manoeuvring him onto a barge.

Then I found one floating. Quizzical,
she unnerves me with her doll's squint.
Washed of river slime, the little idol
is placed on my window sill.

Sometimes, on a windless dusk in autumn
when I open the casement,
she sings softly in Latin,
the pale notes moving like candlelight
out over the Laguna Morta to the dead.

Andrew Nightingale

THE FALLOW YIELD

The old man hummed quietly in the cool shade beside a
watchtower of sorrow, winding the last burnished yarn of
summer onto a skein. In the crowing breeze tambourine leaves
turned slowly to autumn, and sated geese flew swollen into a
prodigal spread. The old man paused for a moment, rested his
song, and briefly read the gnarled journal of his worn hands as
a stranger. 'Soon the river will flow too fast, and become too
cold to bathe in', thought the old man, as he felt the soft twine
slip through his fingers, 'and I will taste nothing but the flavour
of winter'. In the mewing distance a crimson veined evening
purred, and bedded unfurled claws into the fraying skyline.
As the old man continued to reflect on the passing season, a
white mule laden with apples appeared at his side.
The white mule affably extended a cordial salutation, which the
old man, although unable to remember any previous encounter
with the mule, returned with the warm, easy grace of a fond
acquaintance. 'I have often glimpsed you from afar, standing
atop the tower, old man,' the mule began, 'and each time have I
attempted to understand the purpose of your surveillance.'
The old man would have preferred to remain alone and
continue to fix the thread of his broken melody, but he felt
awkwardly answerable to the mule's amiable gaze and
accordingly scratched his grey bearded chin pensively, allowing
himself a few uncomfortable seconds to form his reply.
'Every day I have climbed this lofty tower and watched. But I
am a foolish old man and my vision is dimming. Each sunrise I
see less than I did the sunset before, and I watch little but the
day receding from my grasp,' he lamented, at once feeling

ashamed of his complaint.

'What do you wish to see, old man?' the white mule posed, with a sympathetic smile.

'The expected. Or the unexpected. It makes no difference,' sighed the old man. 'What I wish to see I shall not, and I must settle for any view in its absence.'

Crickets clicked chattering heels, and a peel of cattle bells clanged a languid chorus to accompany the late afternoon's slovenly passage.

'Once I looked out onto a colourful distance which seemed to stretch endlessly into the blue sky, and everywhere I looked I saw myself threshing grain, herding sheep, fishing clear streams. But now I look upon a distance which has caught up with me and I am unable to find myself there.'

'You hoard your sadness as a sleepless old man gathers over-ripe fruit from the tree of dreams, with no thought for the usefulness of his harvest,' the mule advised, shaking its head softly to and fro.

The old man fell silent for a moment and thought hard on the white mule's words.

'My harvest feeds me well enough. I am an old man and I need nothing more than I can take without reaching.'

'You eat the fruit within your reach, yet the fruit is bitter and you complain of its flavour. How does this satisfy you?'

'I am satisfied by the memory of how it once tasted, even though it has become unpalatable to me now.'

'You have grown fat on your sorrow, old man, perhaps you would care to walk with me for a while, and I will show you a sweeter fruit ripe for the picking.'

The old man thanked the mule gratefully, but made no attempt to stand. 'Perhaps I will find a sweeter fruit of my own soon,' he mused, as he watched the mule retreat.
'Farewell then, old man,' bid the whie mule, turning and beginning to walk slowly away. 'I have a long journey ahead, and I must not delay. But I shall remember you well, and I shall think of you often. And I shall see you always in an endless distance, regardless of my station, or whatever view lies before me.'

Chris Tutton

SUMMER-HAIKU

For Frank and Marian Scott

Silence

and a deeper silence

when the crickets

hesitate

Leonard Cohen

ON THE SHORELINE

I have come to love the fisherman's upturned boat,
sea-weed darkened. I walk on the shingle.
A tree without branches grows on the shoreline –
further inland the dog-rose.

I've forgotten a truth I once knew –
at a harp without strings the harpist flounders.
The music is there in the ache of my body,
in words beyond this night.

Wendy French

THE CRICKET

You wished, you wished, you wished in vain.
The August wedding stung with rain.
The dreadful mother lived too long.
The business shrank from his first dream
To crumpled bills at one a.m.
The child said 'See you!' then was gone.

Gaze in the garden's tiny sphere:
You thought it was the hedgehog's year,
Who snuffled plates. Mating or killed,
He disappeared. And butterflies?
Only one peacock's sun-filled eyes
At noon. But when dusk's breath was held

There crouched, upon the roses' bank,
Bronze grasshopper, a tiny tank.
The metal wings were not for fight.
Three more, as by a Southern sea
Whirred, clinked and throbbed, sang constantly,
Gave all you wished, through August's night.

Alison Brackenbury

MUSIC

When music sounds, gone is the earth I know,
And all her lovely things even lovelier grow;
Her flowers in vision flame, her forest trees
Lift burdened branches, still with ecstacies.

When music sounds, out of the water rise
Naiads whose beauty dims my waking eyes,
Rapt in strange dreams burns each enchanted face,
With solemn echoing stirs their dwelling-place.

When music sounds, all that I was I am
Ere to this haunt of brooding dust I came;
And from Time's woods break into distant song
The swift-winged hours, as I hasten along.

Walter de la Mare

SCHUMANN AT MIDNIGHT

He sits at the piano, where a sliver
Of yellow light
Winds through a maze of shadows; she, on covers
Cool and white.
The bedroom floods with music, and she shivers.

His shoulders square against her are a wall
She cannot scale.
But from behind his stiff-backed silence spills
A different tale,
One she knows the movements of too well.

Here are the high, fine, thrilling notes, cross-grained
Against the dark,
And here, the thread that binds them and explains
The chords that part
Far off and found again; part, and are found again.

Katrina Porteous

LIKE CASABLANCA

This is where beautiful friendships always begin
And the usual suspects are rounded up,
Where the private getaway plane is waiting
For the two of us, just a kiss and a small step
Across the tarmac. But hurry, that jeep
Will arrive on cue, and the mist we were lost in
Thicken to night and fog. And then what hope
For the last-minute take-off, for anything?

How exquisite the nostalgic ache, the promise
That suddenly a song will be remembered
In a bar in Berlin or London or Paris
Where we'd met by chance, where we heard
The news of what would become of us
And you smiled as you told me not to believe a word.

John Mole

RAIN BIRD

Are you listening to the rain in our dream?
It is the many thousand languages
Whispered from ghost to ghost and time to time,
Our earthly messages: *can you hear me?*
Are you still there? How close can I hold you
So I no longer know where my skin ends
And yours begins? How can I let you go,
And how say goodbye? Then a night bird
Tunes up in his grove of shadows to the hushed
Tiers and gods of the city in the dark
And quiet rain; *'He sounds lonely'...* 'Shhh –
It's a rain bird, he only sings when it rains; listen ...'
So we do, and he does, and his music
Precipitates the first light, and he's gone.

Nick Drake

JERUSALEM (from 'Milton')

And did those feet in ancient time
Walk upon England's mountains green?
And was the holy Lamb of God
On England's pleasant pasture seen?

And did the countenance Divine
Shine forth upon our clouded hills?
And was Jerusalem builded here
Among these dark satanic Mills?

Bring me my bow of burning gold!
Bring me my arrows of desire!
Bring me my spear! O clouds, unfold!
Bring me my chariot of fire!

I will not cease from mental fight,
Nor shall my sword sleep in my hand,
Till we have built Jerusalem
In England's green and pleasant land.

William Blake

THE FASCINATING CHILL THAT MUSIC LEAVES

The fascinating chill that music leaves
Is Earth's corroboration
Of Ecstacy's impediment –
'Tis Rapture's germination
In timid and tumultuous soil
A fine – estranging creature –
To something upper wooing us
But not to our Creator –

Emily Dickinson

STANZAS FOR MUSIC

There be none of Beauty's daughters
With a magic like thee;
And like music on the waters
Is thy sweet voice to me:
When, as if its sound were causing
The charmed ocean's pausing,
The waves lie still and gleaming,
And the lull'd winds seem dreaming.

And the midnight moon is weaving
Her bright chain o'er the deep,
Whose breast is gently heaving
As an infant's asleep:
So the spirit bows before thee;
With a full but soft emotion,
Like the swell of Summer's ocean.

Lord Byron

APRIL SARABANDE

We two-stepped in the shadow of
The wrecking ball,
Photographing the dance hall with
A confessional eye;
Tossing the timber caber of a
Chance remark
Into the weeping wish that
We had retained
Just one splinter in the palm.

Chris Tutton

HOW OFTEN DOES IT HAPPEN

that every silver thing is turned to gold
    that reservoirs and railways burn like copper
in the dark of winter's infra-red

that frost is fire, and forests
    are a nerve-machine of birch and blood,
that for a few hours all falls quiet

as wind drops like a child in sudden sleep
    and earth's hair stands on end,
that in the amnesty of moon's blind eye

the world confesses to the stars
    those secrets it would rather hidden
in the deep red ocean of electric dark?

Jane Draycott

(after Scott Kahn: *Lunar Eclipse,*2010)

NEAR BUT FAR AWAY

She wavered, stopped and turned, methought her eyes,
The deep grey windows of her heart, were wet,
Methought they softened with a new regret
To note in mine unspoken miseries,
And as a prayer from out my heart did rise
And struggled on my lips in shame's strong net,
She stayed me, and cried "Brother!" our lips met,
Her dear hands drew me into Paradise.

Sweet seemed that kiss till thence her feet were gone,
Sweet seemed the word she spake, while it might be
As wordless music -- But truth fell on me,
And kiss and word I knew, and, left alone,
Face to face seemed I to a wall of stone,
While at my back there beat a boundless sea.

William Morris

A SONG FOR ST. CECILIA'S DAY
November 22, 1687

From harmony, from heavenly harmony,
This universal frame began:
When nature underneath a heap
Of jarring atoms lay,
And could not heave her head,
The tuneful voice was heard from high,
"Arise, ye more than dead."
Then cold, and hot, and moist, and dry,
In order to their stations leap,
And Music's power obye.
From harmony, from heavenly harmony,
This universal frame began;
From harmony to harmony
Through all the compass of the notes it ran,
The diapason closing full in man.

What passion cannot music raise and quell?
When Jubal struck the chorded shell,
His listening brethren stood around,
And wondering, on their faces fell
To worship that celestial sound:
Less than a God they thought there could not dwell
Within the hollow of that shell,
That spoke so sweetly, and so well.
What passion cannot Music raise and quell?

The trumpet's bold clangor
Excites us to arms
With shrill notes of anger

And mortal alarms.
The double, double, double beat
Of the thundering drum
Cries, hark! the foes come:
Charge, charge! 'tis too late to retreat.

The soft complaining flute,
In dying notes discovers
The woes of hopeless lovers;
Whose dirge is whisper'd by the warbling lute.

Sharp violins proclaim
Their jealous pangs and desperation,
Fury, frantic indignation,
Depth of pains, and height of passion,
For the fair, disdainful dame.

But oh! what art can teach,
What human voice can reach,
The sacred organ's praise?
Notes inspiring holy love,
Notes that wing their heavenly ways
To mend the choirs above.

Orpheus could lead the savage race;
And trees uprooted left their place,
Sequacious of the lyre:
But bright Cecilia raised the wonder higher;
When to her organ vocal breath was given,
An angel heard, and straight appeared,
Mistaking earth for heaven.

Grand Chorus

As from the power of sacred lays
The spheres began to move,
And sung the great Creator's praise
To all the bless'd above;

So when the last and dreadful hour
This crumbling pageant shall devour,
The trumpet shall be heard on high,
The dead shall live, the living die,
And music shall untune the sky.

John Dryden

TWILIGHT

How to begin my song?
Two geese fly over
creaking a love song,
But how shall I begin?

Blackbird calls up the garden
then darkness comes rattling,
owl swings low over meadow –
hide rabbit, hide.
I will begin.

Rose Cook

THE MAGIC FLUTE

To begin with we stare into the huge nothingness
exposed by boards, flies, wings, wires,
Not even a feather floating in a shaft of light.

Grey figures appear and sit cross-legged
as if at a loose end. How to hold onto belief
that colour and voice will bloom in this place?

Sound shimmers in the darkness, a figure
in princely red strolls beneath silken clouds. Soon
he's falling in love with the portrait of a princess

and we are in love with the music, the enchantment
it threads. But what are those shadow sets
of shapes shifting restlessly on the backdrop?

We make out heads, shoulders, arms and it dawns:
we're watching our rustling selves. A spotlight
travelling the stalls chooses a girl in white.

Cloaked in our longing, she edges her way
to the aisle, crosses a bridge over the orchestra pit.
The moment hands crown her with ringlets

all of us shed the ordinary's tight skin,
follow the path into fairytale's wood, join
in the difficult search for truth. The flute's tune

protects flesh and breath from any harm
when we undergo trials of fire and water.
Our throats melt as song unites the lovers for ever.

But the heroine takes off her flaxen wig,
the hero folds away his velvet jacket.
Hand in hand they cross the bridge, turn back

into us trailing inadequate selves, clutching
at seedpearls as we weep for wrinkles,
wreckages, the stage empty again.

Myra Schneider

SKIMMING

You can never see what's just around
the river bend: best to let the stone spin
from your palm by chance. Take a little control
by a flex of the knee and a squat stance,
feet planted on wet sand.
Fix your gaze on a mid point
in the current's still centre. Skim
the flattened oval out with a flick
of the wrist. Live fully for that bounce –
one, two, three across the water like a song,
a trajectory of grace before sinking
into the mud where that old pike lurks,
sensing your every move.

Anne Caldwell

A POLAR CAROL

Ice-locked, gripped by a groaning floe,
Fingers numb on my old banjo
As the Northern Lights put on their show.

Snow all around me
And more snow.

From the blinding dazzle of an endless sky
Where time has forgotten how to fly
I send you the jewel of a cormorant's eye.

Goodbye, my love,
Goodbye, goodbye.

My breath is a wreath, a ghostly ring,
And my song already vanishing
Is all I can offer, is everything.

Listen to the silence.
Hear it sing.

Dulce in dulci jubilo,
Frostbite plucks at my old banjo,
Home seems a million years ago.

And snow keeps falling
Snow on snow.

John Mole

TARANTELLA

Do you remember an Inn,
Miranda?
Do you remember an Inn?
And the tedding and the spreading
Of the straw for a bedding,
And the fleas that tease in the High Pyrenees,
And the wine that tasted of tar?
And the cheers and the jeers of the young muleteers
(Under the vine of the dark verandah)?
Do you remember an Inn, Miranda,
Do you remember an Inn?
And the cheers and the jeers of the young muleteers
Who hadn't got a penny,
And who weren't paying any,
And the hammer at the doors and the Din?
And the Hip! Hop! Hap!
Of the clap
Of the hands to the twirl and the swirl
Of the girl gone chancing
Glancing
Dancing
Backing and advancing,
Snapping of a clapper to the spin
Out and in --
And the Ting, Tong, Tang of the Guitar.
Do you remember an Inn,
Miranda?
Do you remember an Inn?

Never more;
Miranda,
Never more.
Only the high peaks hoar:
And Aragon a torrent at the door.
No sound
In the walls of the Halls where falls
The tread
Of the feet of the dead to the ground
No sound:
But the boom
Of the far Waterfall like Doom.

Hilaire Belloc

question

something's out there
      listened for   not heard
something like song
      plucked from a bird

the bird in mind
      is looked for   not seen
an astonishing idea
      among the green

the green's not there
      but named in the head
something growing
      unsayable   unsaid

some things   some notes
      are never found
how   without these
      should the music sound

Clare Best

FRANK SINATRA POEM

I read of Frank Sinatra
Out fishing on the sea
And at the time I felt a rhyme
Was surely meant to be

Perhaps the crooner on the schooner
Was fishing for some tuna...

But the vessel was a yacht
So maybe not.

Marvin Cheeseman

WONDER IN THE NINETIES

As the sun broke through the clouds
I mouthed "ah" in wonder and then wondered
about the "ah" that wonder induced.

The vowels were the seven planets
for Gnostics – the sustained tones
of infinity shaping the universe.

But Gnostic wonder dissipates into
systems. Then reason picks over the cadaver.
Consonants peck, habitual scavengers.

Rimbaud called vowels "silent pregnancies"
and added the usual plosives and fricatives
to bring a poem to birth.

I started to think wonder a shibboleth,
a coterie of those who like to see a certain way.
Interpretation is the revenge of the intellect,

says Susan Sontag. That revenge became
a palace of shock and awe – horror as wonder.
The nineties are a lost cause:

no-one reads the Gnostics these days.
The sustained note was released – my "ah"
crossfaded with nostalgia, the longing

to stay where the universe had shape,
back in the nineties, when my only crimes
were sentimental votives to wonder.

Andrew Nightingale

AERODROME

Don't talk of the words that were lost on the wind,
the multitude prone on the tarmac, his voice
like the voice from a distant echoing cave,
our one hundred thousand cheap lighters raised
like an answering beacon, the uncanny shimmer
surrounding his head, the death of the moon.

Remind me instead of the tongues of fire
we saw by the roadside that night, the visions
that curled like snakes from our tangled hair,
the veteran flight-sergeant, burning coals
in his eyes, who stopping to give us a ride
told us *Write of the things thou hast seen*

and drove down the A31 on the flaming wings
of an eagle, our low hills and dark world revealed.

Jane Draycott

REBETIKA

It was late at night – did she dream it?–
How he led her through the streets in her nightdress,
Barefoot over broken glass
To a rough pub like a secret:

Cigarette smoke, firelight, beer,
Knackered old soaks nursing their grievances
At the narrow English bar;

And leaving her there, returned, minutes later,
Towing a paper-chain of girls – his teenage daughters
Arm-in-arm with their friends. Then a sudden breeze

Blew in from afar, from the Fens, from across the ocean
That carried them, spellbound, to that moment

When, out of the dark, four figures
Step forward, and the air thrills –

Bursts into strings, drums, whirling, stamping feet;
And throwing his arms wide open
He gives it to them as a gift –

The rebellious, wild music of the mountains.

Katrina Porteous

SONNET 8

Music to hear, why hear'st thou music sadly?
Sweets with sweets war not, joy delights in joy
Why lovest thou that which thou receivest not gladly,
Or else receivest with pleasure thine annoy?
If the true concord of well-tuned sounds,
By unions married, do offend thine ear,
They do but sweetly chide thee, who confounds
In singleness the parts that thou shouldst bear.
Mark how one string, sweet husband to another,
Strikes each in each by mutual ordering,
Resembling sire and child and happy mother
Who all in one, one pleasing note do sing:
    Whose speechless song, being many, seeming one,
    Sings this to thee: 'thou single wilt prove none.'

William Shakespeare

IN THE BLEAK MIDWINTER

In the bleak midwinter, frosty wind made moan,
Earth stood hard as iron, water like a stone;
Snow had fallen, snow on snow, snow on snow,
In the bleak midwinter, long ago.

Our God, Heaven cannot hold Him, nor earth sustain;
Heaven and earth shall flee away when He comes to reign.
In the bleak midwinter a stable place sufficed
The Lord God Almighty, Jesus Christ.

Enough for Him, whom cherubim, worship night and day,
Breastful of milk, and a mangerful of hay;
Enough for Him, whom angels fall before,
The ox and ass and camel which adore.

Angels and archangels may have gathered there,
Cherubim and seraphim thronged the air;
But His mother only, in her maiden bliss,
Worshipped the beloved with a kiss.

What can I give Him, poor as I am?
If I were a shepherd, I would bring a lamb;
If I were a Wise Man, I would do my part;
Yet what I can I give Him: give my heart.

Christina Rossetti

"Song, though, is a uniquely human business"
Don Paterson, Poetry Review, Summer 2007

Have you told the blackbird
who wanders air
on walnuts by the yard
the rough farm where
pines sigh above the gun's reach, or
in lilacs by our workshop's broken door?

As the sparks leap and fade
he tries and trails
a note, a run, a glide,
as one sun fails
he steals, then builds; long runs; a phrase
from brother's, father's, grandfather's lit days.

He will not cough or croup
he pours each note
lost trees, each sweep and swoop
gold from his throat.
Idle in sun, pierces dawn's sky
high as the rain's rush. Song? Blackbird, reply.

Alison Brackenbury

ON THE AERIAL

Starling is numerous, holds in his throat
The many colours of his oily coat.
Each year he – like his fathers – finds new noise,
Wolf-whistles tall as boys,
The phone's trill, then the shriek
of Kirsty, loudest child in all our street.
Tonight he softly mews. Then through his voice are poured
Jay, blackbird's honey, thrush-lilts. He, half-heard
Tilts at faint stars, is spring, is every bird.

Alison Brackenbury

IF LOVE WAS JAZZ

If love was jazz,
I'd be dazzled
By its razzmatazz.

If love was a sax,
I'd melt in its brassy flame
Like wax.

If love was a guitar,
I'd pluck its six strings
Eight to the bar.

If love was a trombone,
I'd feel its slow
Slide, right down my backbone.

If love was a drum,
I'd be caught in its snare,
Kept under its thumb.

If love was a trumpet,
I'd blow it.

If love was jazz,
I'd sing its praises,
Like Larkin has.

But love isn't jazz.
It's an organ recital.
Eminently worthy,
Not nearly as vital.

If love was jazz,
I'd always want more.
I'd be a regular
On that smoky dance floor.

Linda France

ONWARD CITY MOMENTS

Onward city moments
        with your all-concerning paths
Your disconcerting crime-rate
        and your public swimming baths

With your traffic flowing slower
        than your gutters and your drains
With your concrete, your congestion
        and your stubborn understains

Onward city moments
        with your teeming seedy charm
Your naked neon night-spots
        and your early morning calm

Onward city monuments
        I bow my humble head
Before your effigies in tribute
        to your high-achieving dead

I praise the public servants
        who keep your channels clean
And lubricate the moving parts
        of your obese machine

Onward city moments
        ever onward on your way
With your cast of motley millions
        pulling through another day

Matt Harvey

ODE TO A POP SINGER

He strutted around the stage like
Christ on gullibles.
They clapped, he smirked, but
No-one noticed.
'I understand he's very religious'
Said a cynic to her friend in
A quiet moment.
'Oh?' replied the friend, swooning to a
Well rehearsed toss of the head,
'Yes, I believe he worships himself.'

Chris Tutton

WILD GARLIC

through the sandstone bridge, she said
flows the river Spey
where the wild garlic grows
won't you come and play?

let's play tickle trout, she sighed
whispering like the river
I would said I, *but...can't be late*
back home for me dinner

yet homewards over the mossy wall
she handed me some fruit
a granny smith turning red
at all her talk of juice

all her talk of juice was like
a philtre drunk at bed,
it made me dream a freckled trout
was standing there instead

a freckled trout standing there,
androgynous, divine
singing of the liquid bliss
together we would find

together we would find, she sang
fluttering her gills,
the love that breathes in silver streams,
a love for which you'd kill

a love for which you'd kill – I mused
it filled me full of doubt,
sung beneath the weeping beech
by a brown and greedy trout

a brown and greedy trout, she was
in a sequin dress
that shimmered round her swinging hips
in whisperings of bliss

whisperings of bliss that told
how – on the other side
things are more than they seem
girl   river   trout

Mark Gwynne Jones

ON THE BEACH

ocean
the sea speaks green here
and mauve and mussel-blue

her arms, her foam-flecked lips

her words are rock, are flick
of fish, sway of wrack, whale-song –
one long syllable, vast as night

shore
I have come back to the language
of stone and sand; my voice
laid out like the ribbon horizon
drinking the sky.
                    The footprints
are mine; the words unimportant.

                    It is time.
The stones climb the hill;
winter peppers the shore.

Wait for moonrise; first star
and a single curlew piping the night.

sky
the night of falling stars

one perfect round quartz pebble
a syllable, a god's eye
clear as early love –

we bring it home, a memory –
all night on the windowsill
it sings its pure white note

and outside all the sky, listening

Roselle Angwin

LUNAR ECLIPSE

The Exe froze over
and the music of the city was hushed.

You watched
the male swans bunch together

in a moon-shaped space of open water
and held your son close to your chest.

Upstream, Leda let her coat slip
from her shoulders onto snow.

She walked out
                of her own free will
to meet that quilled rush of air.

You both stared at her footsteps
in the river-ice and drew each other closer.

Above your heads, a wedge of birds
hooted over and over and over.

Anne Caldwell

AT REMENHAM

for Matt & Louise

Lift an oar from off the water. Wipe the shadow
from the moon. Raise a head from off its pillow
or a coal-pail from the snow. Take all these things away
and what is left's a perfect *oh* or love – a loop,
a ring, an eye to turn the world the right way up,
a guiding lens for tracking stars when far at sea.

It's the path around a sundial, a circle made of stones
where things happen once and yet were always so.
Both centre and circumference, both spy-glass
and the moon, whichever way you turn it, it's the focus
where the fire at the heart of all things burns.

Jane Draycott

AULD LANG SYNE

Should auld acquaintance be forgot,
And never brought to mind?
Should auld acquaintance be forgot,
And auld lang syne!

Chorus:-
For auld lang syne, my dear,
For auld lang syne.
We'll tak a cup o' kindness yet,
For auld lang syne.

And surely ye'll be your pint stowp!
And surely I'll be mine!
An we'll tak a cup o' kindness yet,
For auld lang syne.
For auld, &c

We twa hae run about the braes,
And pou'd the gowans fine;
But we've wander'd mony a weary fit,
Sin' auld lang syne.
For auld, &c

We twa hae paidl'd in the burn,
Frae morning sun til dine;
But seas between us braid hae roar'd
sin' auld lang syne.
For auld, &c

And there's a hand, my trusty fere!
And gie's a hand o' thine!
And we'll tak a right guide - willie waught,
For auld lang syne.
For auld, &c.

Robert Burns

ACKNOWLEDGEMENTS

'Cello Suites', 'Cusp' and 'On the Beach' by Roselle Angwin from "Looking for Icarus" (Bluechrome) 'Corn Dryer, Struggs Hill' by Clare Best from "Treasure Ground" (Happenstance 2009); 'question' by Clare Best from "Excisions" (Waterloo Press, 2011); 'lullaby without voices' by Clare Best first published in "The Rialto" no. 70 Autumn 2011 and "Excisions" (Waterloo Press, 2011) 'Left' by Alison Brackenbury has been published in the "Warwick Review". 'Song, though, is a uniquely human business' has been published in "Poetry Review". 'On the Aerial' by Alison Brackenbury was published by Shetland Libraries poetry posters for their 'Bards in the Bog' project and in 'Shadow' a chapbook from Happenstance Press, 2009. 'Sunday Morning - Chichester Cloisters' by Anne Caldwell has been published in "Dead Ink" 2011. 'The Wholesomeness of Coldplay and their Fans' by Marvin Cheeseman has been published in "Best of Manchester Poets". 'Frank Sinatra Poem' by Marvin Cheeseman from "Full Metal Jacket Potato" (The Bad Press). 'Summer Haiku' from "The Spice Box of Earth" by Leonard Cohen, published by Jonathan Cape. Reprinted by permission of the Random House Group. 'Rain Bird' by Nick Drake from "From the Word Go" (Bloodaxe Books 2007) 'How Often Does It Happen' by Jane Draycott first published in International Gallerie (India) Issue 27, 2010. 'Aerodrome' first published in "The Captain's Tower" (eds Bowen, Furniss, Woolley) Seren Books 2011. 'Billie Holiday at Carnegie Hall' by Linda France from "The Simultaneous Dress" (Bloodaxe Books 2002) '52nd Street' and 'Blues for Bird' by Linda France from "Storyville" (Bloodaxe Books 1997) and 'If Love was Jazz' by Linda France from "Red" (Bloodaxe Books 1992). Reprinted by permission of the author. 'On the Shoreline' by Wendy French has appeared in the "Poems in the Waiting Room" chapbook. 'Play' by David Hart: Numbers 1,3,5 from "All Saints Elegies" published in part in "Leviathan Magazine" and the whole in "The Republic of Letters" (Boston, USA 2003) and "Running Out" (Five Seasons Press, 2006). 'Footprints' and 'Onward City Moments' by Matt Harvey from "Where Earwigs Dare" (Green Books) 'How Strange the Pain' by Matt Harvey from "Songs Sung Sideways".

'Lallation', 'I am Lifting the Piano with One Hand' and 'Jig' by Gaia Holmes from her second collection "I am Lifting the Piano with One Hand" (Comma Press, 2012). 'Wild Garlic' by Mark Gwynne Jones from "Psychicbread" (Route 2003). Musical renditions of 'Wild Garlic' and 'In the Light of This' appeared on the CD: "In the Light of This" (Route 2006). 'From River Sounding' by Mimi Khalvati from "Child: New and Selected Poems" (Carcanet Press 2011) The long sequence 'River Sounding', from which these two poems were extracted was published in "The Long Poem Magazine" (2011) 'The End of Time' by Mary MacRae from "As Birds Do" (Second Light Publications, 2007) 'The Woodcarver' by Andrew Nightingale from "The Big Wheel" (Oversteps Books; www.overstepsbooks.com) 'The Artist at 81' by Lawrence Sail from "Waking Dreams: New and Selected Poems" (Bloodaxe Books 2010). 'The Silence in the Garden' by Myra Schneider from "Circling the Core" (Enitharmon Press, 2008). 'Mahler's Ninth' by Myra Schneider has been published in "Artemis Poetry Issue 4" 'The Magic Flute' by Myra Schneider from "Multiplying the Moon" (Enitharmon Press, 2004) 'Pearl' by Myra Schneider from the sequence "Core - Circling the Core" (Enitharmon Press 2008) 'Piano Solo' from "In Dr No's Garden" by Henry Shukman, published by Jonathan Cape. Reprinted by permission of the Random House Group. 'Trumpeters' from "In Dr No's Garden" by Henry Shukman, published by Jonathan Cape. Reprinted by permission of the Random House Group Limited. An earlier version of 'Writing to Some-one Else's Music' by Hannah Silva was published by Tears in the Fence. 'Live Within This Music' by Hannah Silva has previously been published in "Intercapillary Space" 'Symphony', 'Questions for all Ages', 'The Fallow Yield' and 'April Sarabande' by Chris Tutton from "Seasons of Winter" (Avalanche Books, 2005) 'Ode to a Pop Singer' by Chris Tutton from "Acnestis in Elysium" (Avalanche Books 1995)

8P 3/13